BREAK A LEG!

AN ACTOR'S GUIDE
to Theatrical Practices, Phrases and SUPERSTITIONS

Meticulously and Most Impressively
• COMPILED BY •
SUE MINER *and* MARK BROWNELL

Break a Leg! An Actor's Guide to Theatrical Practices, Phrases and Superstitions
First published 2011 by
J. Gordon Shillingford Publishing Inc.

Cover design by Elliot Smith
Interior design by Relish Design
Edited by Ruth DeGraves and Glenda MacFarlane
Author photo by Lily Miner-Brownell

Printed and bound in Canada on 100% post-consumer recycled paper.

We acknowledge the financial support of the Manitoba Arts Council and The Canada Council for the Arts for our publishing program.

J. Gordon Shillingford Publishing Inc.
P.O. Box 86, RPO Corydon Avenue
Winnipeg, MB R3M 3S3
Canada

Library and Archives Canada Cataloguing in Publication

Brownell, Mark
    Break a leg! : an actor's guide to theatrical practices, phrases and superstitions / Mark Brownell and Sue Miner.

ISBN 978-1-897289-64-8

1. Theater—Humor. 2. Actors—Humor. 3. Superstition—Humor.
4. English language—Terms and phrases—Humor. I. Miner, Sue
II. Title.

PN6231.T57B76 2011   792'.02907   C2011-903123-X

Foreword

Q: What did one rocket scientist say to the other?
A: Hey, it's not theatre!

Sometimes theatrical knowledge is acquired not through formal education but by picking things up along the way. And so unique words, phrases, and stories are passed down to us from the previous generation of performers…and then the cycle begins all over again. This book is the culmination of a combined seventy years in the business. It is humbling to think that most of it is collective knowledge that has been passed down for centuries. *It is a very old profession after all.*

Is it completely comprehensive? No. We see this book as a living document. There are sure to be some missed opportunities here and we count on you the reader to contact us so that we can add forgotten phrases and corrections to future editions. It's not meant to be a tome. We have also only scratched the surface of some of the definitions. This book is only an accessible and handy reference guide. We have also chosen to leave out a portion of technical terms that do not directly concern actors. (Believe us. It's safer that way.)

If we offend, it is with our good will…

A true lexicographer will always avoid editorializing as he or she compiles and defines words. But we wanted a book that entertains as well as informs. And so, sprinkled throughout the text are bits of arcane knowledge, superstition, etiquette, and opinion that we want to pass down. Some of the content is tongue-in-cheek. Some of it one may not agree with. But all of it has some truth at its core.

Special Thanks: Glenda MacFarlane, Marcia Johnson, William Vickers, Andrew Boutilier, Jane Moffat, Maev Beaty, Donny Osman, Alan Williams, Michael Mawson, Brian Way, Dorothy Davis, Violet Walters, Hilary Unger, Chris Earle, Shari Hollett, David Craig, Guillermo Verdecchia, and all our splendid colleagues over the years who have taught us about all this stuff…and how it's not rocket science.

A

A-frame – a ladder used for hanging lighting instruments.

above the title – when the star performer's name appears prominently before the title of the play in programmes, advertisements and marquees.

accent – adopting a foreign dialect to create a character. While it's totally fun and somehow makes access to choices easier, it can be abused. (See "crutch.") Also note, if one is actually going to be among people who speak the way one is pretending to (ie: Scotland) it is fully wise to hire a dialect coach.

acoustics – the quality of sound transmission from the stage to the audience in a particular building.

act – 1. (noun) an essential structural division in a script. There may be up to five acts in a given play. 2. Also as a verb: "To Act" upon a stage. 3. Acting: The art, profession, or activity of those who perform in stage plays, motion pictures, etc, to play out a story.

act curtain – the curtain closest to the proscenium which, when opened, reveals the playing area to the audience. Also called front curtain, main curtain, working curtain, or grand curtain.

acting area – the area of the stage where the play is performed. Also called the playing area.

actor – theatres and restaurants are full of them.

actor-manager – an actor who also runs the company in which he/she appears.

actress – a female performer in a play. Most actresses prefer to be called actors.

ad-lib – abbreviation of the Latin *ad libitum* "freely, as desired". To improvise lines or speeches that are not part of the script. Ad-libs are often used to cover miscues, as many actors are want.

affective memory – a Method technique involving the invocation of past experiences in an actor's life in order to help him to recreate genuine emotion on stage.

agent – an actor's intermediary who performs various matters of business connected to the theatre such as contracts, pay scale and auditions. Theatrical agents are increasingly a rarity these days. Most agents now only handle television, film and commercials work. If starting out, be sure to find a reputable agent. Anyone who asks the actor to pay huge amounts of money upfront should be avoided. A good agent may ask for an administration fee, but beyond that they get paid when the performer does. Usually, a theatrical agent makes 10% of the actors fee.

alienation effect – a much-abused and misunderstood Brechtian technique that stipulates the emotional detachment of both the audience and the actors from the drama, in order to emphasize the intellectual significance of what is happening. Too often used as an excuse for a sloppily staged play. "But I *wanted* it to be completely incomprehensible! It's alienation!"

amateur – someone who loves what they do in the theatre but receives no payment for his or her work. Can also be used as a derogatory term meaning unprofessional.

amphitheatre – *(ancient Greek)* a circular, semicircular, or elliptical auditorium surrounded by raised seating.

amplifier – A piece of equipment which increases the sound captured by a stage microphone. Or boosts the sound replayed from a record, CD, or tape.

angel – a financial backer with deep pockets.

animals (and children) – never act with them. (W.C. Fields) Notorious for scene stealing because they are so truthful and cute.

antagonist – the principal character in opposition to the protagonist of a drama. Traditionally thought of as the villain, the antagonist has the advantage of always moving the plot forward and is therefore an integral part of the play.

anticipate – to jump or telegraph a cue, joke, or moment on stage. Anticipation is a common acting error that adversely affects the believability of a scene.

applause – the actor lives for this.

apron – in the traditional theatre, the part of the stage which projects in front of the curtain. In many theatres this can extend over the orchestra pit.

arbor – a metal frame that holds counterweights.

arc – the principal plot of an ongoing storyline in the episodes of a narrative; the continuous progression or line of action in a story.

areas – the divided portions of the stage used to apportion the lighting design.

arena stage – a stage in which the audience is seated on all four sides. Also called "theatre in the round." Yes, even if the space is still square, so to speak.

artistic director – the artistic and administrative head of a theatre. With the guidance of a board of directors and full knowledge of a theatre's budget the Artistic Director plans the season, is crucial in fundraising and grant preparation as well as hiring guest directors and creative teams. The irony of the modern day artistic director's role is that it has very little to do with art or directing. He/she is in charge of selecting plays but not necessarily directing them. Also, ADs are key to a theatre's community profile. Some artistic directors have a reputation for being socially awkward but only as a result of being constantly deluged by eager actors looking for work.

aside – a remark addressed to the audience which other characters in the scene do not hear or notice, often used when the audience needs to be let in on something the other characters don't know.

assistant director – an apprentice who assists the director. The exact role of the assistant director is entirely dependent on what the director wants from him or her. The task may take the form of taking notes, directing lesser scenes and transitions, or simply going on coffee runs. It can be a thankless job or a very useful opportunity to observe rehearsal.

Assistant Stage Manager (ASM) – often general stage-hands. Never underestimate them.

"What were you thinking?!"

Superstition: Never marry the ASM.

audience – public attendees of a play. Also called "punters" and "bums in seats." Spectators.

audition – a competitive test between actors vying for one part. The process of letting producers and director know one is the best actor for the role/job.

auditorium – the part of the theatre where the audience sits. Also known as the House.

auguste – a clown term. Auguste is an archetypal idiot savant character. His foil is "Joey" who is a bossy know-it-all clown. Together they make up a classic manipulator/victim duo. Auguste will often get the better of Joey at the end of a sketch.

avant-garde – a modern dramatic movement that reacted against realism, favouring a more imaginative and unconventional approach to theatre.

B

back drop – a large piece of canvas hung from a batten and painted to represent a particular scenic element. Also called a drop, a back cloth, or scrim.

backstage – the area behind the stage, including the dressing rooms and the green room. Also called "offstage."

backstage lights – dim blue lights used during a performance for crossovers, often called "running lights." So the actors can see.

backing flat – a flat which stands behind a window or door in the set.

balcony – a gallery of audience seats that projects over the main floor in a theatre or auditorium. Sometimes cheaper, although balcony centre is often the best seat in a proscenium house.

banjo – a rail along which the curtain runs.

bar – 1. an aluminium pipe suspended over the stage on which lanterns are hung. 2. Also a drinking establishment (See "with the fairies.").

Bard (The) – there is only one "Bard" in Theatre. Actors will often call William Shakespeare "The Bard" or "The Bard of Avon".

barker – someone who talks up a show outside of a theatre.

barn door – an arrangement of four metal leaves placed in front of the lens of a spotlight to control the shape of the light beam.

barnstormer – an actor who performs in a noisy declamatory style.

batten – a bar made of wood or steel from which scenery, lights, or curtains may be hung and flown in and out. Also called "Pipe".

beard role – an older character. King Lear, Prospero, Polonius, Santa Claus etc…. archetypal.

beat – a pause for effect. Also a self-contained sequence of text. There are two possible origins for this term. It may be borrowed from musical terminology or it may be derived from Stanislavski's distinctive pronunciation of the word "bit" as in "break the scene into little bits". An actor understands a beat in a scene.

beginners – those members of the cast who are on-stage when the curtain goes up. The call "overture and beginners" is a signal to the orchestra to start the introductory music and for the cast to get into position on-stage.

being in the moment – being in character spontaneously and truthfully.

belt – to sing loud. A "belter" is a stage singer who specializes in volume and duration rather than finesse. (See "Ethel Merman.")

benefit – a special performance of a play where the box office receipts go towards a charity.

best show in town – the one we are in. It is always important to convince oneself and others of this.

between gigs – unemployed.

bio – short for biography. A short description of one's theatrical experience used in the press release, program or lobby display. Often used to thank family and friends who have possibly been ignored because the actor has been in rehearsal.

birds – it is unwise to act with a live one of these onstage. Even the meekest of birds will feel the unquenchable desire to sing its head off once the curtain goes up. (See also: "animals and children.")

bit – stage business or a short beat.

blackout – switching all stage lights out at once, leaving the stage in complete darkness. (See also "DBO.")

blacklight – ultra-violet light that illuminates phosphorescent paint. A physical guide for the players.

black box – an empty stage or set with a black floor and black walls either hard or fabric. Often fringe and festival venues provide a black box to enable multiple companies and artistic needs.

blacks – 1. black curtains at the back and sides of the stage. 2. Also, technicians wear black clothing to minimize their visibility onstage during scene changes.

blocking – 1.the choreography of the actor's position and movement on stage during rehearsals. Occasionally known as plotting or staging. 2. Also an improv term where a performer prevents a sketch from establishing itself. Example: "I heard that you just got married." "No, I didn't." (see also: "yes and…") 3. Blocking may also refer to one actor getting in the way of another: "You are blocking my light".

blue fairies – blue rinse crowd, an audience made up of seniors—who quite often make up a large portion of the audience for weekday matinees.

board – another name for a control panel for lighting or sound.

boards – the stage. "Treading the boards" means to act on the stage.

boat truck – a movable platform, upon which a component part of the set can be wheeled onto the stage or, alternatively, raised up to it from below.

bomb – a production that is perceived to be terrible and without merit, hence affecting the box office money making potential. (See also: turkey, flop, dog.)

bond – a sum of money posted by a theatre to Equity to guarantee actors' salaries.

boo! – traditional vocalization of disgruntled audience members. Sometimes encouraged in melodramas and Christmas pantos when the villain enters. (See also: "Hiss!")

boo birds – audience members who boo.

boom – vertical freestanding pipe to hang lighting instruments. Also called a "light tree".

book (the) – a copy of the script kept by the Stage Manager, which includes all cues and notes. Also known, usually in amateur theatre, as the "prompt copy." 2. May also refer to the text sections of a musical score.

book ceiling – a hinged ceiling made from a pair of flats.

book flat – two flats hinged together in order to be self-supporting when folded partway.

book wing – an arrangement of attached wings capable of being revolved so as to present a different scene, turning like the pages of a book.

boom stand – a microphone stand which has an angled arm.

booth – the room wherein the technical aspects of a show are controlled. Usually at the back of the house, though the British sometimes have the stage manager call the show from backstage left.

borders – scenic material hung at the top of the set to hide the fly system from the audience. Also called teasers.

bought house – an actor will sometimes get a more lucrative television or movie gig during the run of a show. Rather than bring in an understudy there may be a provision for the actor to purchase all the seats in the house so that there will be no performance.

box office – the place where tickets are sold. Also used colloquially to mean the size of the audience ("What's the box office like tonight?")

box set – a set which consists of three walls, around a proscenium arch stage. The proscenium opening is the fourth wall. Also known as a "room set."

brace – a length of wood used to support a flat, usually held in place by a sandbag.

break out of character – when an actor drops out of his role onstage.

breakaway – a prop that is specifically made to break at a certain point in the play.

breaking curtain – to visibly cross the stage when the house is open in pre-show is considered very bad form.

break a leg! – a pre-show greeting. Traditionally means "Good Luck!" Possibly from the tradition that if you bow so long your leg will break. Or you have to "break" the narrow wing drapes (legs) to get onstage and take your bow. Or you have to break (bend) your knee to bow.

breaks – very important. Equity has rules about them. Dinner breaks, coffee breaks, etc, during the rehearsal period. Time between shows during runs.

breakdown – 1. Any list that itemizes—a costume breakdown lists costume pieces required for each scene, etc. 2. Also, as a verb, to "break down" a costume or set piece means to make it look used by soiling it slightly or fraying the edges.

Brechtian – using (or abusing) the theatrical conventions of German playwright Bertolt Brecht. (See Alienation)

bridge – an extension of the flies, capable of being raised and lowered in order to facilitate work on lighting and scenery. Also: catwalk, elevator.

"Big Bang Beginning"

SUPERSTITION: **A very old way to begin a performance went like this: The stage manager came out before curtain and rapidly banged an inverted broomstick on the stage thirteen times—followed by three extended bangs. Obviously, this will get the audience's attention...but it also appeases the theatre ghosts, banishes evil spirits and frightens away any vermin.**

---

bums in seats – the paying audience.

bun head – a ballerina.

Burlesque – a racy performance style combining songs, sketches, striptease and variety acts. Not surprisingly, Burlesque survived longer than the less sexy Vaudeville. 2. Also, in Britain a Burlesque is a spoof of a more serious play.

business – (or stage business)—a particular piece of staging or manipulation of props that has been choreographed.

busker – a street performer who makes a living passing a hat. Or bottling as known in Europe.

butterflies – stage jitters. Pre-performance anxiety. Some actors pee their pants in the wings.

C

c-clamp – a curved piece of metal used for fastening lanterns to a lighting bar.

cabaret – an intimate show combining music and various forms of theatre at a club or other venue. Often the audience is seated at tables and drink while watching the show.

cable – electrical cord used in circuiting lighting instruments or other stage devices requiring electricity.

call – an instruction to the company usually given by the stage manager. A rehearsal call is an instruction to attend a rehearsal at a particular time. Time calls are given just before each performance ("Ladies and gentlemen, this is your thirty minute call."). Etiquette note: When a stage manager gives one a time call, be sure to acknowledge with a "thank you". A treasury call (British) is a pay-day in the professional theatre. See also "The Half".

call-back – an invitation to return after an initial audition. Sometimes there are many call-backs. Some directors see this as an opportunity to work out staging ideas before rehearsal actually starts. If one isn't getting paid, don't let people abuse this courtesy. Three call-backs are more than enough. See also: cattle call.

call board – the bulletin board at a rehearsal hall or theatre where the stage manager posts the schedule of the day for scene work, costume fittings, photo-calls, and interviews. During a show's run, actors may be asked to sign the sign-in sheet on the call board when they arrive at the theatre.

call for a line – when an actor forgets a line in rehearsal he/she will ask the stage manager on book to repeat it. This is done by saying "Line?" "Yes?" and in extreme cases "Well what is it!!" If one doesn't actually call for a line the stage manager will remain silent as you may be "acting".

calling the show – the stage manager does this from the booth. He/she advises the sound and lighting operator when a technical cue is coming. ("Stand by Light Cue 254.") Nothing happens until the stage manager says "Go".

CAEA – Canadian Actors Equity Association. See "Equity." Union membership to guarantee proper wages.

cans – headphones.

cast – 1. (noun) the list of characters in a play and the actors who play them. 2. Also as a verb: to allocate parts to members of a company.

casting call – a general request for actors to audition for specific rolls in an upcoming production.

capsule review – a brief critique in a newspaper or online.

caster – a small wheel used on scenery and scenic equipment for ease of shifting.

catharsis – *(ancient Greek)* the emotional release experienced by the audience, ideally achieved at the end of a tragedy. Also purgation.

cattle call – a general audition where anyone can show up without an appointed audition time.

catwalk – an immobile platform above the stage that reaches from one end of the stage to the other. Used to gain access to the hanging stage equipment.

cauldron trap – a square trap positioned upstage—so-called from its use in the witches scene in *Macbeth*. Many a cauldron trap has malfunctioned and injured people -- thus feeding the *Macbeth* curse.

cellar – the area beneath the stage used for storage and access to the stage through traps.

centre line – an imaginary or real line that divides the stage area into two equal parts, running from downstage to upstage.

centre stage – the middle of the performance space.

chair theatre – a one-man show that features no set—except for a single rehearsal chair in which the performer sits and the audience listens to a monologue.

character – a stage role that the actor plays.

character actor – someone who specializes in doing non-leading roles. These may be comic relief or beard roles etc. Smart leads approach their parts as character actors.

cheat – a staging term. Playing to the audience but retaining a realistic scene presence. Example: an actor who carries on a dialogue with another actor while facing slightly downstage is said to be cheating to the audience. See also: proscenium style.

check your props – the ASM will often set the props, putting them in the starting positions for the show. When they ask one to check their props it is very advisable to do so. This seems obvious but, in the heat of the moment, good pre-show prep can prevent a major stage crisis.

chewing the scenery – extreme overacting.

child wrangler – a stage-hand who babysits child performers backstage. Also called a chaperone.

children's theatre – a theatrical performance geared towards a young audience. Many actors who perform in children's theatre think of it as "paying your dues" because of harsh working conditions touring school gymnasiums with rowdy students first thing in the morning. Children's audiences are notoriously fickle—though some would call them the most honest audience one will ever have. See also the culturally modernized "Theatre For Young Audiences" and "Youth Theatre."

choreographer – devises and rehearses the dance routines, following the concept discussed with the director.

choreography – staged movement, dance, or combat.

chorus – a group of actors who support the main roles in a production. Often seen in dance numbers and crowd scenes mumbling "Rhubarb, rhubarb". A Greek theatrical device.

circuit – a set group of theatres that are regularly visited by theatre companies.

clapper – two planks of wood hinged together that produce a loud sound offstage. A much more reliable and safe method for creating a gunshot effect than relying on a gun that fires blanks onstage.

clap trap – provoking "spontaneous" applause on stage by pandering to the audience. Clap trappers are shameless self-promoters and fellow actors are often amazed of the clap trapper's gift to arouse applause in every show they are in.

climax – a decisive moment that is of maximum intensity or is a major turning point in a plot. This is often a misunderstood term in theatre. The climax is best thought of as the turning point where the characters, their world, and situation are never the same afterwards. It is followed by a conclusion in the play.

claque – *(French traditional)* a group of paid audience shills who clap and generally talk up the play. The claque will not just applaud – but will also tell people to shush when a particularly great stage bit is coming up. There is also the "anti-claque" who is paid to boo rival performers. The use of paid shills dates all the way back to the infamous public presentations of the Emperor Nero (AD 54 to 68).

clippings – vain actors often carry around good reviews in their wallets/purses and will dig them out at a moment's notice. "Have you seen my clippings?"

closing night – the last show. An opportunity to over-indulge in food, sentimentality, and drink before going on to the next theatrical adventure.

cloth – backdrop scenery painted on fabric. Cloths can be on a banjo (usually in the amateur theatre), can be rolled up, or can be flown.

clown – we could write an entire book about this word and the phrases and traditions surrounding it. Clowns have been around for centuries. The word is thought to be derived from "clod" – a ball of dirt.

It is a very humble origin indeed. In the Dark Ages clowns were often just the village idiot—someone to boot around and make fun of on your way to market. They are the lowliest and poorest of performers but they are also the primal and archetypal force behind the development of character and comedy. Their misery is our entertainment. The fear of clowns "coulrophobia" is a very real and intense psychological condition.

Types of Clowns:

Baby Clown – a classroom exercise that "births" a student's new clown.

Balloon Clown – (derogatory) an untalented amateur who slaps on the face paint and scares children at birthday parties or tries unsuccessfully to cheer up patients in hospitals.

Bouffon – A separate and far more disciplined and respected form of European clowning.

Shakespearean Clown – often the least funny character onstage.

Tent Peg Clown – classic American circus clown. P.T. Barnum referred to them as the "tent pegs" of his business.

clown nose – a little red plastic or foam ball that attaches to the nose. Some people believe that wearing one of these will make them funny.

clown stop – a comic interlude on stage while a set is changed.

coarse acting – amateur overacting. An essential and entertaining book on this topic is *The Art of Coarse Acting* by Michael Green. (The best book in the world about what not to do.)

coffee – so necessary for a morning rehearsal. If one sees the coffee maker empty and know people will want more, make some. One will be much loved by the ASM.

cold reading – a reading of a play or scene without any preparation. Sometimes done at auditions and call-backs.

colour changer – a remotely controlled means of changing a coloured filter over the lens of a lantern. There are three kinds: a wheel, a semaphore (like the old- fashioned railway signals) and a scroller that uses continuous, usually dichroic, filters. Scrollers are the preferred option in the modern theatre.

colour frame – a frame which fits over the front of a lantern to hold a coloured filter or gel. They can be made from metal (preferred) or a kind of cardboard.

colour wheel – a metal disc fitted with small circles of coloured gel, which when rotated in front of a spotlight produces a succession of differently coloured beams.

comedy – an intentionally funny play. Often accepted to be the hardest style of theatre to perform.

comedy of manners – a witty comedy that satirizes social mores.

comps – free (complimentary) tickets.

command performance – performing for a monarch.

come down – in the theatre, a show does not finish; it comes down, i.e. the curtain "comes down" to end the show.

Commedia del Arte – a comic theatrical tradition with a set of stock archetypal characters that evolved in Italy during the 16th century. Its lively improvisational comic nature continues to influence the theatre to this day.

comic relief – a character part that is used to perk up the audience and/or to buy time for a quick costume change. (The Porter in *Macbeth* accomplishes both.)

community theatre – amateur theatre – local companies of actors who perform plays and musicals without being paid. More recently: artists who gather with members of a community to workshop and perform a creation based on local history.

composite setting – a stage setting in which three or more different locations are presented simultaneously on stage.

conflict – dramatic discord of action, feeling, or effect between characters. Conflict is usually caused by characters with competing desires. Inner conflict can also arise within a specific character. (Hamlet is a very good example of this.) Dramatic conflict is a primary element of theatre. Without it there is no drama and the audience will quickly lose interest. Integral to plot.

contact sheet – the address book of a production comprised of sheets that contain the phone number, and email address of everyone on a show. These sheets are sometimes broken down and given out by department.

convention – the rule or rules for the universe of a given play. ie, Actors speaking directly to the audience from the beginning of the play creates a convention for that play. Stage conventions can be broken but it must be done deliberately and with great care. It can be done with lighting and music as well, as a stylistic device.

copyright – the legal entitlement of the owner of a dramatic work to claim a fee known as a royalty. To perform a play without the permission of the playwright is illegal, unless it is a work in the public domain such as a play by Shakespeare.

corner – (*British*) short for the "prompt corner"; the place from which the stage manager controls the show. From here he/she has communication links to all parts of the theatre and gives cues to all departments. The corner can be on either side of the stage but traditionally it is on the left (i.e. the prompt) side. Perversely, some theatres have the prompt corner on the "opposite prompt" (OP) side of the stage. The person who is operating the corner is sometimes said to be "in the corner" and sometimes "on book."

cornerblock – a piece of 1/4" plywood cut in the shape of a triangle, used to connect the stile to the rail on a flat.

corpsing – when an actor breaks out of character and laughs. Highly unprofessional (yet fun to watch.) Fellow players can induce this helplessly.

costume – onstage wardrobe.

> ### *"Costume Conundrum"*
>
> **SUPERSTITION: Costumes should never be worn in public. Also, it is bad luck to wear a new costume in a remount. Also, if a costume catches on a piece of scenery then the actor must retrace his steps and make a new entrance or face dreadful hoodoo for the rest of the show.**

costume designer – a person responsible for creating or procuring the wardrobe and prop items that are essential to the costumes of the characters in the performance. A costume prop might include a fan or purse.

costume fitting – measuring, adjustment of costume with dresser and designer. It is a time to discuss specific movement needs that may not have been considered in the design and will affect the practicality of the costume. If one has a costume fitting they must be professional and shower beforehand...and wear underwear.

costume parade – a time when the director and designer sit in the house and watch the actors try on each costume under stage lights. This time also useful to do any movement that one's character makes to ensure the costume behaves. Also called a "dress parade."

costume plot – a list and description (breakdown) of every costume piece worn by every actor in a play. Often an actor will be given a dressing room "cheat sheet" list of costumes needed for changes during the show.

costume sketch – the costume designer usually creates a two-dimensional drawing of the character in costume for the director's perusal. Actors are fond of procuring these after a production and framing them. However, one's character is always one's own.

cotton mouth – stage jitters can cause various symptoms. Cotton mouth occurs when the saliva in your mouth dries up completely and you are unable to speak your lines. Strangely, the jitters can also cause too much saliva—resulting in wet showers of spit flying into other actors' faces, or even into the audience.

counter-mask – playing the exact opposite of what might be expected from a character in a specific scene. (ie, a very old character will act youthful.)

crash – showing up to an audition without being formally invited. Crashing is usually an acceptable practice in the theatre so there is no need to feel like one is imposing. Crashers are often slotted into vacant positions left by actors who don't show up. That said, there is no obligation for producers to see them.

crash box – a box filled with metal or glass that is shaken to create offstage sound effects.

crash 'n burn – the very first run after the scenes have been blocked. It's usually pretty messy. Similar to assembling pieces of cut cloth on a table and knowing it will be a beautiful garment soon.

crew watch – a rehearsal where the stage crew is invited.

critic – the bane of every actor, playwright and director; the person who writes reviews of theatre performances. Many actors will claim that they do not read reviews. Traditionally critics have a very stormy relationship with those that they critique. If they are too nice they may be labelled as pushovers or boosters. If they are too nasty they can expect lots of ad hominem threats and insults in return. It is a well-known fact that bad reviews sell more papers than good reviews. But bad reviews can also affect advertising dollars from the theatres that they slam. With so much stress and conflict involved a critic will often burn out and move on to another section of the newspaper.

Robertson Davies once said that critics "only write for and about themselves". Brendan Behan wrote, "Critics are like eunuchs in a harem: they know how it is done, they've seen it done every day, but they are unable to do it themselves."

These days the role of the professional critic is in question with the proliferation of social media, bloggers, and alternate methods of attracting an audience.

critique – (derogatory) a snooty review.

cross – a staging term. To move from one area of the stage to another.

crossfade – fading from one lighting state to another.

crossover – the backstage pathway between stage left and stage right.

crush bar – drinks are served here in the foyer. Called the "crush" because the audience often mobs it during intermission.

crutch – (derogatory) a stage gimmick that an actor uses to establish and maintain a character. These include accents, limps, prosthetic humps, club foots, hairy moles, cigarettes, walking canes, eye-patches, stuffed parrots on shoulder, etc. Crutches are sometimes used to good effect at the beginning of rehearsals, and are then cast away as character work progresses. Everything in measure though.

counterweight system – a type of rigging that uses weights to counterbalance horizontal battens containing scenery, curtains, or lighting equipment.

cube tap – a three way electrical connector (looks like a cube)

cues, technical – each sound and lighting effect is called a cue and is given a number, level, and timing. These are all plotted well in advance of the technical rehearsal.

cues, visual – often technical cues are called on an actor's movement rather than a line. So the stage manager will wait for the actor to cross up to the window before the thunder and lightning happens. Because of this, actors often invite the ire of the stage manager if they change their blocking to suit their emotional state.

cues, text – stage managers expect exact line readings during a performance. They rely on actors to know their lines and repeat them accurately. And, of course, actors depend on cues from other actors.

cue light – specific light used by the stage manager to cue backstage technicians and actors. Normally, when turned on functions as a warning and when turned off signals "Go."

cue sheet – the page(s) used to note the cues given by the stage manager to different technicians.

cue-to-cue – a rehearsal where the stage manager goes through each technical cue. Actors are asked to pick up a scene at a certain line, go to a certain line, then stop. This allows the stage manager and operators a chance to rehearse their sound and lighting cues before embarking on a technical run.

curtain – in addition to its normal definition relating to draperies, a term used to indicate the start or end of a performance such as "Five minutes to curtain."

"Curtangled!"

SUPERSTITION: A tangled curtain drop is considered bad luck for the run of a show.

curtain call – taking a bow in front of the audience at the end of a show. Sometimes abbreviated to "curtain". Usually rehearsed at the end of the dress rehearsal.

"Calling all Curtains!"

SUPERSTITION: It is bad luck to block the curtain call during early rehearsals.

curtain line – 1. the line on the stage floor where the front curtain touches when brought in. 2. The final line in the play. (Also called the "tag line.")

curtain music – music played while the curtain is closed, usually before a performance begins. Also known as pre-show music.

curtain-raiser – a short play presented before the main drama. Might also be called the "warm up act."

curtain set – a set made entirely of curtains—replacing flats.

curtain speech – a brief speech given before the performance begins. Often delivered by the Artistic Director; it is a chance to welcome the audience, tell them of upcoming events and 50/50 draws, as well as to advise the ever important cell phone reminder.

curtain up – a stage command that begins the show. Also "curtain out" (for curtains that draw to stage left and right).

cut of the box – professional actors who are not on a full Equity contract will often just take a share of the box office profits. (If they are wise they will ask for a gross cut. If they are unwise they will agree to a net cut after expenses.)

cut off line – an unfinished line that needs to be cut off by another actor or cue.

cut-out – a free-standing piece of scenery. Example: a 2-dimensional tree cut out of board and painted.

cyc lights – type of powerful lighting instruments used to light the cyc with a smooth wash.

cycle – a series of plays with a continuing storyline and characters.

cyclorama – usually shortened to "cyc". A very large piece of white fabric, tensioned on two or more sides, which covers the entire back wall of the stage. It can be lit in various colours or have slides or gobos projected onto it. Also: a curved drop or wall used as a background to partially enclose the set. Quite often used to depict the sky. May be painted or lit.

D

dame (the) – (*British*) the role of the Pantomime Dame stretches back to the earliest origins of the theatre when female characters were played by boys and men. The tradition continues to this day with plays like *The Importance of Being Earnest* where Lady Bracknell is more often than not played by an older male actor.

dance captain – a member of the company who can rehearse choreography with the company after the show has opened.

dark theatre – a day or night when there is no performance. Often either Sunday or Monday.

dead house – 1. a lacklustre audience. 2. Also, stage acoustics with very little echo. A full house will deaden the sound coming from the stage.

deck – the stage level, derived from ship terminology.

dénouement – the settling action just prior to the final resolution of the intricacies of a plot.

design – the visual and visceral concept of the show created from conversations between the director and design team (set, costume, lighting and sound).

deus ex machina – (*from ancient Greek*) the God that came down and saved the day when the plot had twisted itself into a knot. The "machina" was a stage crane that lowered the actor from above or below. Used now to describe a too-convenient plot resolution.

dialect coach – a teacher of accents and proper pronunciation. Not to be confused with a voice coach.

dialogue – conversation between two characters in a play. Also: The lines or passages in a script that are intended to be spoken.

diction – proper onstage pronunciation. Some actors spend a lot of time on their appearance but rarely work on this essential part of stage training.

dim – to decrease the intensity of a stage light.

dimmer – an electrical apparatus used to control the intensity of the lighting instrument to which it is circuited. Found on the lighting board.

dimp – to ruin a moment or scene. (The opposite of "pimp".)

diorama – a set that makes use of special lighting, cut-out scenery, and transparencies to create three-dimensional effects and an impression of movement.

dips – electrical sockets set into the floor of either the stage or the wings, and usually covered by little trapdoors.

director – person at the creative head of a given production. He/she develops the concept of the production then further develops it with the design team and fellow creative team (choreographers, composers, music directors etc.) It is the director's job, in conjunction with the theatre, to cast the actors, attend production and design meetings, and rehearse the play in keeping with the budget and overall perimeters of a given theatre or venue.

direct audience address – a convention of speaking to the audience.

discovered – a person or object on stage when the curtain goes up.

do-fer – a temporary prop used in rehearsal.

dog – a bad play.(See also: flop, turkey, bomb.)

doubling – one actor taking more than one part in a play. In Shakespeare's day, as in King Lear, the role of the Fool would be doubled with Cordelia, thus explaining why they are never on stage at the same time in the script.

downstage – the part of the stage that is closest to the audience.

drag act – character cross-dressing.

dramatis personae – (*Latin*) A list of the characters in a play.

dramaturge – literary facilitator to the playwright. Can act as an editor. Gives advice regarding plot arc, historical accuracy and background characterization, etc. The exact role of the dramaturge is often nebulous and changes depending on a production's needs.

drama queen – a high-maintenance actor of any gender who likes to focus on themselves and the drama of their own lives rather than the drama on stage. Also: "Prima Donna."

drawing room drama – an old-fashioned play with one very formalized set.

dresser – crew person assigned to help with quick changes and general maintenance of costumes throughout the run of the show.

dress rehearsal – the final rehearsal with all the conditions of real performance. It will be non-stop and timing is adhered to regarding curtain up and time of intermission. There may or may not be an audience. (Also: "Dress Tech")

"All dressed up..."

SUPERSTITION: It is said that a bad dress rehearsal means a good first show.

dressing the set – after the set has been physically built by carpenters it may need "dressing" with objects desired by director and set designer to fulfil the design concept. Sometimes, quite literally, decorating the set with stuff.

dressing room – the place where you put opening night cards on your mirror and focus before the show. Actors keep it neat, knowing that they will be otherwise chastised.

drinks after the show – an ancient ritual. A veteran actress once said: "You go out for drinks after the show and look for love." This is because so much love is given in one's performance that one actually feels a bit depleted afterwards. Needing compliments is natural but beware—one will be emotionally vulnerable after a show.

drop – a piece of scenery or fabric that is raised or lowered in performance.

drop box – a box that holds a falling prop (such as the dead bird in *The Seagull*) suspended from the flies. It is wise to keep a duplicate prop that can be thrown onstage from the wings in case the drop box malfunctions.

dropped line – a missed bit of text.

dropping character – when an actor stops acting onstage.

dry – a verb: an actor who forgets his words is said to "dry". In performance, an actor who dries is often saved by another actor jumping to a fresh cue. (One must buy that actor drinks after the show.) Also called: brain freeze, brain fart, caught in the headlights.

dry tech – running the sound and lighting cues without actors.

DSL – down stage left. Towards the front of the stage on the left-hand side as one looks at the audience.

DSR – down stage right.

dumb show – a brief pantomimed play or tableau that tells a story without using words.

duologue – a play with only two actors delivering lines.

dying – (onstage) means giving a very poor performance. (Which really feels like dying.)

E

ego board – lobby display of headshot pictures and bios of actors.

ego trap – compliments or a good review. One must be careful, not to take these too seriously—one does one's work.

eight by tens (8" x 10"s) – photos of the actor for self-promotion and lobby display. Some actors succumb to vanity and use very old eight by tens for their resume shots. This is unwise. One should always have a resume picture that reflects one's current appearance.

emote – (derogatory) to express emotion, especially in an excessive or theatrical manner.

Empty Space, The – the influential book by world-renowned director Peter Brook. A blueprint for a stripped down modern theatrical practice that rejects traditional ways of making theatre.

encore – (*French*) "again". In theatre, an extra curtain call.

ensemble – a group of performers who work together.

ensemble piece – a play that depends on the strength and teamwork of a group. Often the parts are of roughly equal importance.

enter/make an entrance – to move into the stage acting area.

"Trippingly on the Tongue"

SUPERSTITION: To stumble upon entering the stage is considered very bad luck.

entrance line – the first line of text upon entering the stage.

epic theatre – a form of Brechtian political theatre based on an appeal to the intellect rather than to the emotions.

epilogue – a brief scene or speech given at the end of the play.

equity – the shortened form for Canadian Actors Equity Association or CAEA, the association for professional actors. Equity enforces the rules of professional conduct, contract agreements, and pay.

escape stairs – the steps, unseen by the audience, that an actor uses to "escape" after an upper-level exit; also used to get in place for an entrance from upper platforms or doors.

etiquette – there is a strict code of conduct in the theatre that has been handed down for generations. A few examples of theatre "rules":

- the show must go on
- punctuality is essential
- never miss an entrance
- always give one's best regardless of the size and composition of an audience
- never miss a curtain call
- never take notes from anyone but the director or stage manager
- never leave the theatre during a performance
- avoid temperamental outbursts
- be gracious when accepting praise and stoic when receiving criticism

- do not speak badly of a play when in rehearsals or during the run
- do not gossip
- handle all props and costumes with great care
- observe backstage courtesy and deportment

exeunt – (*Elizabethan stage direction*) one or multiple characters exit the stage.

exeunt severally – multiple characters exit the stage in different directions.

exit line – last line spoken before exiting stage.

exit – a stage direction—moving out of the acting area, going offstage.

exposition – text that tells a lot of plot information without a great deal of drama. A playwright's greatest challenge is keeping the exposition down to a minimum. It can be done by sugar-coating it with dramatic action.

extro – in musical theatre the music played at the end of the curtain call as the audience is walking out. If one is still in the theatre at the end of the music, do applaud enthusiastically for those musicians.

F

facilitator – an alternate term for director. A facilitator may have less overseeing control than a director.

fade – sound and lighting term: to increase (fade up), decrease (fade down) or eliminate (fade out) gradually the brightness of a lantern or the volume of a sound.

falling action – the part of a dramatic plot that occurs after the climax has been reached. The action falls towards resolution of the plot. See also denouement.

false ending – a moment near the end of a performance when the audience mistakenly thinks the play is concluding. False endings are caused by bad writing and/or bad directing. Example: a poorly timed blackout that is too close to the final curtain.

false proscenium – a constructed proscenium that fits inside the permanent proscenium.

farce – a form of comedy characterized by broad humour, outrageous characters and complicated plots. Comedy has been described as featuring normal characters in outrageous situations, whereas farce gives us outrageous characters in normal situations.

feed – giving someone a line. It could mean setting up a gag or providing a line to someone who has dried on stage.

fifth business – a character that arrives in the last (fifth) act of a Shakespearean play to restore order, mop up the blood, and tie up the plot's lose ends (Fortinbras in Hamlet).

fight director – the person who stages, with an eye for safety, and the actors' ability to repeat the actions, any fight scenes, combat, duels, etc. (Also: "Fight Choreographer.")

fight captain – a member of the company who conducts rehearsals of the fights each night before the show.

fill light – lights used to illuminate shadowy areas.

finding your light – being able to ascertain where to stand in order to be lit to maximum effect at a particular moment. See also "hitting your mark."

fire! – It is unwise to yell this in a packed theatre. See: Mr. Sands.

fire curtain – a non-flammable curtain hung directly behind the proscenium that protects the audience from fire or smoke emitting from the stage. May be the same as the Act Curtain. Also called Asbestos Curtain or Fireproof Curtain. Important for an actor to know location as it will automatically drop in the case of a fire alarm, and it is very heavy.

fire marshal – the theatrical equivalent of the Boogie Man. The Fire Marshal has (thankfully) never understood the phrase "The show must go on".

fire proofing – Sometimes costumes and set have to be sprayed with a fire retardant, usually done if a character is dealing with cigarettes or any kind of flame on stage.

fire regulations – a big deal in theatre with all the hot lamps in the lighting grid.

first electric – the first row of lights hung on a batten behind the proscenium.

flash-pot – a small box that will cause a noisy explosion of smoke when ignited. Not to be checked by putting one's face into one. Seriously.

flash paper – quick burning flammable parchment used as a stage effect.

flat – an oblong frame of timber, covered with either canvas or hardboard and painted, which forms part of the set. There are also door flats, window flats, even fireplace flats. Canvas flats, being lighter and easier to move around, are the preferred option, but schools often go for hardboard-covered flats that are more durable.

floater – a line of text that is so bad or difficult to say that it stands out in the text.

flood – a floodlight: a lantern which gives a wide-spreading, unfocused beam of light. These can be symmetric (i.e. casting the light equally in all directions) or asymmetric (casting it more in one direction than the others). The symmetric flood is probably the cheapest stage lantern and the least useful.

flop – a bad play that closes quickly.

flop sweat – that cold, clammy sensation when one realizes that a performance is going poorly and one feel disliked. Advice: continue dialogue but stop acting. Just get through until one is in the moment once again.

flowers – flowers are commonly placed in the actor's dressing room as an opening night gift.

"Aaaaaachoo!"

SUPERSTITION: Real flowers should never be used onstage. This is more common-sense than superstition thanks to allergies.

flub – a dropped or messed up line.

fly – verb: scenery which is raised into the roof (flown out) or lowered on the stage (flown in). The apparatus for doing this consists of a series of ropes and pulleys in the "fly tower" (a very high roof space) and they raise or lower the scenery by means of a counterweight system or by directly pulling on "hemp lines". The men who operate the "flies" are called "flymen" and the area in which they work is called the "fly floor" of, quite simply, the "flies." People can also be flown (a la Peter Pan) in a harness.

fly gallery – a platform that runs above the stage on one side, used in the operation of fly lines.

fly house – a theatre that uses an automated mechanical fly system

flyman – crew person in charge of raising and lowering the flies.

focus, actor – the actors have to be mentally focused to perform.

focus, stage – the place on stage that the director wants the audience to look at.

focus, lighting – to point the lanterns in the right direction and set the correct beam-spread and edge.

foh/front of house – anything which happens on the audience side of the curtain is said to happen "front of house". The term "the house" is used to mean either the auditorium, or the audience ("We had a good house tonight"), or even the theatre itself. It can also refer to the employees within the house: the box office staff, bartenders, ushers, people who give out programs – all workers who are supervised by the house manager. (Essential support staff.)

foil – a character that makes another seem better by contrast. Example: the straight man was the perfect foil for the comic.

follow-spot – a type of profile spotlight with an iris diaphragm and a handle so that it can be used to follow a performer around the stage in a beam of light of exactly the right size. Traditionally called a "lime": hence the term "being in the limelight". These produce a very bright beam of light which is more powerful than that produced by any other lanterns.

forestage – an extended apron in front of the main curtain.

footlights – 1. A series of lights placed on the stage floor along the front of the stage. 2. Also a term for the theatre in general.

fourth wall – the imaginary wall between the actors and the audience in a conventional set design. An actor "breaks" the fourth wall when he acknowledges the audience. Originated with the convention of a Proscenium stage.

foyer – area of the theatre between the auditorium and the entrance. NB: The bar is often found here.

french scene – a scene that begins and ends with the entrance or exit of a character.

freeze – 1. Paralyzed by stage fright or forgotten lines. 2. Also, freeze tableau games are commonly used in theatre classes.

fresnel – a kind of spotlight in which the light is concentrated by a resnel lens (a lens with concentric ridged rings). Projects a variable angle soft-edged beam. Usually given the French pronunciation, "fre-nel'".

fringe theatre – 1. A form of alternative theatre sprung from the fringes of Scotland's Edinburgh Festival in the 1950s. Fringe Theatre has since spread around the globe. Fringes are non-juried theatre festivals that are open to all applicants. Participating theatre companies will pay a flat fee and will then be assigned performance times at a theatre for the duration of the festival. 2. Also: Low budget theatre, self-produced.

front elevation – a scale drawing that gives a front view of the set.

fx – effects: usually sound effects in the theatre but can also refer to pyrotechnics. In film, usually refers to visual (i.e. computer generated) effects.

G

gaffer tape – heavy silver/grey tape used for everything. In reality it is everyday duct tape but for some reason theatre techies call it "gaffers" and get very indignant when one calls it duct tape. (NB: They also get indignant when one calls them "techies".) If one asks for "gaffer tape" in a hardware store one will be met with confused silence. Then they may point towards the electrical tape.

gag – a joke.

gel – a filter placed over the front of a lantern to change the colour of the light.

general manager – in larger theatres this person is in charge of business affairs of the theatre. Sometimes also called the producer.

gesture – (*traditional*) gesture is the outward expression of what is in the mind, the heart and the soul of the character.

ghost – some theatres do have them, or believed to by thespians.

SUPERSTITION: **Surprisingly, ghost sightings are said to be very good luck for the run of a play. The thinking behind this is that the show is so good that even the spooks want to see it. Ghosts are rarely seen by audiences but "theatre folk" often spot or hear them during the run of a play at the back of the house or in an empty audience box. Ghosts may laugh, applaud or heckle when all else is silent. They are also spotted frequently in rehearsal as passing shadows on the periphery of vision—particular during violent scenes where someone is murdered. They come in various forms: Corporal manifestations or insistent sounds (known as "knocking ghosts"). They also have the telekinetic power to move physical objects such as props, wallets, and even much larger set pieces and lights. (Perhaps not so coincidentally, Theatre thieves have this power as well.) Belief in ghosts is widespread in the acting community.**

ghost glide – a type of trap where an actor standing on a wheeled platform appears to glide across the stage as he is raised up to it through a long narrow stage cut.

ghost light – a bare light left on the stage when the theatre is locked up for the night.

gig – actors sometimes borrow this musician's phrase – a performing job.

glass crash – a sound effect simulating the breaking of glass—usually produced by pouring broken glass and china from one bucket into another. (Also: crash box)

glow tape – marking tape that glows in the dark, placed in small pieces around the set so the actors and crew will not bump into anything during a blackout.

gobo – a piece of metal or glass, which fits into the gate of a profile spot and projects a pattern onto the set. Gobos can be very complex. They are first fitted into a gobo holder. Holders vary in size (each type of lantern requires a different size), although the gobos themselves are of a standard size. Most basic gobos are made of metal but very complex patterns can be created on glass gobos. Also called a "template". The stage effect is sometimes called a "break up."

gods (the) – cheap seats in the upper balcony. (Also: Nosebleeds, Peanut Gallery, Helicopter Seats.)

going to black – general blackout warning call from the stage manager during tech. If one is onstage when this is announced it is ettiquette to acknowledge by saying, "thank you".

good mention – a good review. (also "good notice.")

go – a stage manager's command to execute an effect.

go up – 1. In theatre slang, a show does not start, it "goes up"; i.e. "the curtain goes up at eight." 2. Also a term for forgetting one's lines. (see "dry.")

god-mic – a microphone used by the stage manager to communicate with actors during a tech rehearsal.

gossip – few secrets can be hidden in the Theatre. (See "The Stratford Swivel" and "programmed sound.")

grand guignol – a broad and blood-soaked style of performance based on sensational events, including murder, rape and gruesome talian.

grease paint – old-fashioned oil-based make-up.

grid – a steel framework above the stage from which the fly system is rigged.

grip – crew member who moves scenery.

green room – a backstage room used by actors and crew as a waiting and meeting area. There are many explanations for the term going all the way back to 1599 and the Blackfriars Theatre in England where the "tiring room" behind the stage happened to be painted green. Another theory supposes that green carpet was used on stage for tragedies. Since comedies were far more popular the green carpet was more often stored in the backstage common area. In Medieval days "The Green" referred to the actual stage. The green room was therefore a staging area for performers. It is also possible that green room might be corrupted from "scene room"—a backstage area where scenery and props are kept. David Mamet suggests that it is originally from a British gardening term. The green room is a mud room where gardeners kick off their boots.

Still more unlikely theories:

The green room is painted green because it is a soothing colour.

Many actors suffer from pre-show jitters and their complexion changes to green due to nausea.

The green room is the place where envious lesser actors spend their time trashing the reputation of those onstage.

In Restoration Theatres, the minor players, usually young, less experienced "green" actors, were banished behind the scenes. Hence, the backstage room was for the "green" players and came to be called the green room.

Long before modern makeup was invented the actors had to apply makeup before a show and allow it to set up or cure before performing. Until the makeup was cured, it was green and people were advised to sit quietly in the green room until such time as the makeup was stable enough for performing. Uncured makeup is gone, but the green room lives on.

"Get a room!"

SUPERSTITION: A green room that is painted green is considered bad luck.

grocery list – inconsequential lines of text.

ground cloth – a heavy piece of muslin used to cover the stage floor.

ground plan – a scale diagram that shows where the scenery is placed on the stage floor. Also called Floor Plan.

groundlings – (*Elizabethan*) audience in the cheap, standing-only part of the theatre. Also known as the pit.

groundrow – a row of lights on the floor.

gypsy – a dedicated performer, a chorus dancer.

gypsy house – an audience filled with theatre professionals—sometimes a preview. A very friendly house.

SUPERSTITION: The Gypsy Robe is the traditional presentation of a chorus girl's robe to an actor before the opening of any Broadway musical. The recipient dons the gypsy robe and travels around blessing performers backstage.

H

hair acting – derogatory term for not performing well. (Also: sweater acting, purse acting.)

half (the) – half an hour before the first actors are due on stage (i.e. 35 minutes before the show begins). All actors must be in their dressing rooms by the Half. Traditionally the audience is allowed into the auditorium at that point. In olden days the house manager blew a whistle in the auditorium to announce the Half.

ham/hambone – a serial over-actor. Having too many hams onstage may lead to a turkey.

hand props – objects that are handled by actors during the performance.

hand-off – the action of a crew member handling a prop for an actor at a designated time and place during a performance or an actor passing a prop to someone offstage.

hanging – the process of putting a lighting instrument in its designated spot according to the light plot.

Harold – an extended form of improvisational theatre, or "improv", developed by famous Chicago improv director Del Close.

head of wardrobe – person responsible for the making, repair and washing of all costumes.

headshot – a front-on eight by ten photograph, with the face being the centre of the picture and containing minimal or no surroundings.

hemp house – a theatre that uses manual labour and hemp ropes to fly set pieces.

hiss! – audience heckling usually accompanied by "Boo!" In Pantos, audiences are sometimes encouraged to do this when the villain enters.

hit – 1. A very popular show. 2. A "hit" can also be a decisive/climactic moment in the text of a play.

hitting your mark – being at a specific point on the stage at a specific moment in the play—crucial for lighting.

hold the curtain – to postpone the opening of a show to accommodate late audience arrivals or to deal with a backstage emergency.

hot spot – the area of the greatest illumination projected by a lighting instrument.

hot walker – a non-actor who stands onstage while the lights are focussed. (Also "stage walker.") In French "une crabbe".

house (the) – the part of the theatre where the audience sits. See also FoH.

house is open – this means "everybody get off the stage because the audience is coming in".

house left/right – the reverse of stage right and left. The point of view from the audience.

house lights – lights used to illuminate the area where the audience sits.

house manager – the person in charge of everything which happens front of house (FoH): box office, ushers/usherettes, the bars, cash, etc. The house manager will cue the stage manager that the house is in and the show can begin.

house mix – the sound that the audience hears.

house tabs – the curtains across the front of the stage.

house to half – near the beginning of a performance—a lighting cue dimming the audience house lights down by 50%. This signals the audience that the play is about to start.

hubris – *(ancient Greek)* an arrogant excess of pride that leads the protagonist of a play to inevitable destruction.

I

iambic pentameter – a common rhythmic meter in Shakespeare consisting of an unrhymed line with five feet or accents, each foot containing an unaccented syllable and an accented syllable.

IATSE – International Alliance of Theatrical Stage Employees. Pronounced "Eye-at-see."

IDR – invited dress rehearsal. A rehearsal with a small and friendly invited audience. Often the last rehearsal before a paying preview audience sees a production.

impresario – a producer of theatre.

improvisation/improv – general term for scene work that is created by actors. Often used as a tool in rehearsal to find out history of character and situation.

incidental music – music written specifically for use in a theatrical production without being part of the plot itself.

independent activity – a bit of stage business—like folding the laundry while speaking lines—that makes the actor's performance appear more natural.

indication – (derogatory) a hollow acting style with lots of arm waving, posing and telegraphing of lines. "Showing" rather than "being".

indie – independent theatre. Indie companies are often small and are not affiliated with any larger companies or spaces. Increasingly they are the driving force behind the creation of new theatre.

ingenue – 1. A young woman's role. 2. A young female actor.

inset – a small piece of scenery placed within a larger piece in order to facilitate a rapid change of set.

instrument – 1. A term for lantern, or any lighting device. What in domestic terms we mean by the word "light". 2. Also, an affected actor will often refer his body or voice as his "instrument".

instrument schedule – a list of the types of lighting instruments to be used in a show. Also called a Hookup Sheet or Lighting Plot.

intermission – while the audience gets cookies and drinks, intermission is a strange half-time limbo for actors. They are neither characters nor themselves.

intuition – will never fail the actor.

in the moment – acting with spontaneity. Meisner described this as "living truthfully under imaginary circumstances." It is borrowed from the zen teaching of "mindfulness".

in the round – a stage where the audience surrounds the action with gangways on four quarters.

in rep – (see "repertory")

italian – a spoken run-through of a play at a greatly quickened pace. Meant to sharpen the actors' recall of their lines.

iris – a tin sheet with a small hole cut in the centre. Placed over a wide-beamed lamp to make the beam narrower (also called a donut.)

iron – the safety curtain.

IQ Light – a computerized lighting instrument that can act as a follow spot or special. It can change the location of its focus throughout a performance as programmed by the lighting designer.

J

jack – a triangular-shaped brace used to support scenery.

jack-knife stage – when one or more rostra are pivoted on wheels at one corner, thus enabling them to be swung quickly into and out of the stage area.

"Piece Out."

SUPERSTITION: Working on a jigsaw puzzle backstage during a show is an invitation to miss one's cue. Finishing a jigsaw puzzle during a show is considered bad luck. Someone often hides the last piece to prevent this.

Joey – derived from clown Joseph Grimaldi, who made his first appearance in 1800. (See also Auguste). A joey is a bossy clown character.

jog – a narrow flat, usually between one and four feet wide.

jump – to skip a major portion of text.

jump a cue – to come in early with one's line, especially unfortunate if one treads on someone else's line or business.

K

"Regicide!"

SUPERSTITION: Period plays are filled with king characters. After a run, cast and crew often feel it necessary to perform a mock ritual killing of an actor who plays a sovereign. Supposedly this is done to deflate the actor's bloated ego.

---

kitchen sink – (derogatory) a drama that hopes to capture true life by representing everyday action on stage. Boringly realistic theatre.

"A Likely Yarn."

SUPERSTITION: Knitting onstage is thought to be bad luck by some.

L

ladders – high stands for hanging lanterns at the side of the stage. Does not hold the weight of a person.

lamp – the part of a lighting instrument that emits the light; the "light bulb" of the instrument.

lav – a cordless lavalier microphone pinned to the actor's costume, or worn somewhere on the head or face. In musicals actors need to be "laved up" usually by a stage hand.

laying an egg – giving a really bad performance.

lazzi – from the commedia dell-arte—lazzi are bits of comic stage business that do not forward the plot.

lead – main character of a play.

legs – 1. Narrow curtains or cloth that hang vertically on the sides of the stage to mask the backstage area. Also called Tormentors. 2. Also: a show that has "legs" is thought to be worthy of a long run.

Leko – a type of lighting instrument that emits a hard-edged circle of light. Known by its brand name. Also called an Ellipsoidal Reflector Spotlight (ERS) or Profile Spot.

level set – a technical rehearsal where levels for sound and light are set by the designers and director.

lighting board – the console that controls all the lighting instruments. Also called the Dimmer Board.

lighting plot – a drawn-up plan that designated the placement of lighting instruments relative to the set.

lighting designer – responsible for designing, focusing and plotting the lighting for a production. In the professional theatre he/she is not normally responsible for operating the lighting.

lighting tree – a vertical pipe that is placed on the side of the stage to hold lighting instruments. Also called "Boom" or a "Christmas tree".

line level – sound term, referring to non-microphone inputs: CD, tape, MIDI.

lines – 1. Spoken text. 2. Also, cords hung from the grid, used to fly scenery and stage equipment.

"What's my line?"

SUPERSTITION: It is considered bad luck to repeat the last lines of a play in rehearsal.

line readings – when a director (or anyone) tells an actor exactly how to say a line and asks for imitation. Sometimes a director will tell the actor which words to stress or even a sketch of the intention. This is okay, but exact line readings to be copied are considered bad form. Giving too many line readings is the mark of a poor or inexperienced director.

line run – a informal pre-performance speaking of the lines. (see Italian.)

lip – downstage edge of the stage.

load-in/out – the time a show goes into or out of a theatre. Large crews are usually assembled just for this period.

loge – the front section (or box) of the lowest balcony, separated from the back section by an aisle or railing or both.

LORT – League of Resident Theatre. A group of Equity theatres around the U.S. that have joined together and created a specific LORT contract. The theatres categorize themselves into LORT A, B+, B, C, and D, according to their box office receipts. Each LORT level has slightly different rules.

luminaires – theatrical lamps.

luvvies – (*British derogatory*) actors who call each other "darling" all the time.

LX – electrics. The title is given to the lighting department, and the Chief Electrician is known as the Chief LX. Lighting cues when written are called LX cues.

lyric – the text of a song in a musical.

M

"Big Mackers"

SUPERSTITION: One could write an entire book on the Macbeth curse and its lasting legacy. This is the most enduring and involved set of superstitions in the Theatre. The play *Macbeth* was supposedly cursed from the start because Shakespeare (that mad genius!) included actual satanic incantations— "toil, toil…", etc. inviting untold evil into theatres around the world ever since. The original Globe Theatre was said to have burned down after *Macbeth's* first performance in 1603. An interesting theory except for the fact that The Globe actually burned down in 1613 during a performance of *Henry VIII*—started by a spark from a stage cannon. But that didn't stop this superstition from growing and mutating over hundreds of years. Initially, producing the play itself was not said to invoke bad luck. In fact, it's one of the Bard's most popular plays. But quoting lines, character names, or the title during production of *other* plays is considered very bad luck and invites actual physical harm (even death) to the offender. One of the more rational explanations for this is that repertory companies would often have *Macbeth* as a standby production if a new show flopped. So any mention of *Macbeth* during a show was bound to provoke suspicion among the cast that things were not going well at the box office. Other variations on this superstition include:

- Do not make fun of the curse.

- Do not even use the phrase "The Scottish Play" or "Mackers" or "That Play" etc. (This curse isn't easily fooled.)

- Do not quote lines, character names, or title in a theatre. This has since been expanded to not quoting anything from Macbeth anywhere on the planet and maybe even in outer space. This is exacerbated by the fact that there are so many famous and memorable lines in Macbeth.

Remedies for bad luck incurred by quoting *Macbeth*:

- The offending actor must turn around three times and spit and/or swear and then beg forgiveness from all assembled.

- The offending actor must leave the room, and ask for forgiveness from the other side of the door.

- The offending actor must leave the theatre entirely and run around the building three times.

- The Lord's Prayer must be recited by a priest in the theatre.

- Holy water must be sprinkled on the stage apron. Etc. etc. etc. And on it goes.

make-up – make-up is subtler today and often street make-up or no make-up is okay.

"Just make it up."

SUPERSTITION: It is bad luck to wear make-up outside of the theatre. This dates back to puritan times in England, when actors were hounded and beaten by religious zealots. Also: it is bad luck to accidentally spill a make-up box. PLUS: it is bad luck to have another performer look at your reflection while you put on make-up.

---

marking – going through the motions of a scene or choreography without performance energy or emotion. Dancers are really good at it because they know how to conserve energy for performance. Singers also will go through something without using full voice.

maroon – an electrically fired flash, set off in a steel tank fitted with a wire mesh top, to simulate an explosion. These are so loud that it is as well to inform the police in advance if one is to be set off (and at what time), so that they can be ready to deal with hundreds of reports of bombs going off!

mask – 1. to hide or block: an actor masks another when he stands in front of him and prevents the audience from seeing him properly. 2. Also a noun: fabric hiding a row of lanterns hung above the stage. 3. Also: covering used to conceal an actor's face or head usually to achieve some ritualistic or symbolic effect on stage.

masking – 1. to hide any stage equipment or offstage area through the use of curtains, flats, etc. 2. Also to block the audience view of another performer.

matinee – an afternoon performance.

meet the stage – a chance for the actors to check out the set for the first time, walking around through exits and entrances, seeing how far it is to the dressing rooms etc. (Backstage is almost more important because that will be quite dark.)

Melpomene/Thalia – *(ancient Greek)* the mask-holding muses of tragedy and comedy. Just as barbers have barber poles, actors have the much abused and maligned "happy face/sad face" mask symbols of the Theatre. They are an ancient reminder that theatre has its roots in religion.

melodrama – a play that emphasizes sensational plot rather than character or intellectual content.

Derived from musical terminology "melodram" —underscored music that heightens emotional response. Melodrama exaggerates plot and characters in order to appeal to the emotions.

melodramatic – (derogatory) describes overwrought acting.

memory play – a play that jumps back in time as a character reminisces onstage.

metatheatre – theatre that is aware of its own theatricality. There is much confusion and contradiction surrounding this overused term. A few examples of metatheatre in action are: a ceremony within a play, role-playing within a role, reference to reality, self-reference of the drama, and play within a play.

method (The) – American style of acting that uses emotional memory exercises to elicit a truthful performance. Supposedly championed by Stanislavsky but more closely linked to the Actor's Studio of Lee Strasberg. Is sometimes applied in a derogatory manner to describe a self-involved kind of acting.

mic – (microphone) a device that is used to pick up sound for amplification.

mid-Atlantic – a vague British accent approximated by North American actors. Conversely a lot of Brit actors often adopt a western or southern drawl to approximate American speech.

mime – 1. (verb) to use imaginary props. 2. (noun) speechless white-faced clown-like character with striped shirt, suspenders, and flower. 3. A style of speechless performance popularized by Marcel Marceau in the 1950's. Its practice as "pantomime" has been around much longer however dating all the way back to ancient Greece. Over the years popular culture has heaped scorn on The Mime. It is now probably the most despised and cliché performance archetype in the world. Even clowns get more respect. People joke: "Kill a Mime".

miscue – an incorrect cue that triggers a light change, entrance, etc.

mixer – (mixing board) a device for mixing together and modifying sounds from a variety of sources: microphones, tapes, CDs, musical instruments, etc.

moment – an event, big or small, onstage.

monitors – sound speakers.

monitor mix – amplified sound that actors hear onstage.

monodrama – a play in which only one actor speaks. Also: one-person show. Or a "one-hander".

monologue – a portion of text where one character speaks uninterrupted for several lines.

motivation – the internal/psychological reasons or desires for making an acting choice. Sometimes the directorial reply to "What's my motivation?" is "To not get fired."

Mr. Sands – theatrical code to warn theatre employees of a fire without frightening the audience. "Mr. Sands is in the foyer" means that fire has broken out in the foyer.

mugging – (derogatory) bad acting with exaggerated facial expressions. Also called "facial gymnastics" and "face magic."

mummers play – (*European*) an ancient form of folk theatre with roots in primitive ritual.

musical director (MD) – in charge of the musical interpretation of a musical. Working alongside a director, the MD rehearses the singers and musicians, and conducts the orchestra or band. The musical director gives music notes and the director gives acting notes.

N

NAR – No Acting Required. When the actor and character are experiencing the same thing onstage.

Naturalism – a late 19th-century movement in the theatre that reflected a new desire to present an authentic version of "real life"—choosing then-shocking subjects such as divorce and contemporary social mores.

neutral – a state of readiness without contrivance.

neutral mask – a full, white mask in male or female with a neutral expression.

non-Equity – not yet a member of an actor's union. There are various ways to become a member of CAEA or AEA, but it may not be to one's advantage at the beginning of one's career, as there may be less competition for non-Equity roles.

nosebleeds – cheap seats in the upper balcony. (See also: The Gods.)

notes – the observances of a director from watching the work. These are not corrections necessarily but inspiration to go further in the work. If one is given the same note multiple times it may be a communication problem that needs clarification.

note session – happens in a focused way after a run-through of an act or a play. Actors should write down their notes and review them before the next rehearsal or performance.
note etiquette:
    ⋆ *Who can give notes:* The director, choreographer, music director, fight director. The designer can give costume notes but they can't give acting notes. The stage manager can give technical notes and acting notes after the play has opened. Notes cannot be given by anyone other than the stage manager after

the 1/2 hour call is given, and even this should be brief (i.e.; pick up the cues in act one).
    ⋆ *Who cannot give notes:* One's friends, family, agent, the playwright, the producer, one's cat, and most importantly OTHER ACTORS! If there is something driving the actor crazy, it is best not speak to one's fellow actors, speak to the stage manager and it will be addressed appropriately.

objective – what a character wants. (Also related to intention.)

obstacle – whatever is standing in the way of what a character wants.

off book – knowing one's lines. Interestingly, the opposite of off book is not "on book" but "not off book"

on book – when someone offstage is watching the text closely in case someone calls for a line. This is often done by the ASM but can also be requested of other actors. If one is sitting on book give the line promptly and clearly so as not to interrupt the flow.

on your own time – direction meaning "when one is ready but please don't take too long."

one act – a short play with no structural division or intermission. Ninety minutes is thought to be the maximum length that an audience can endure without heading to the crush bar. Producers dislike one acts because they can't sell liquor at the intermission.

one for the pan – like the first crepe that is sacrificed to the frying pan, so is the first run-through of a scene after not having worked it for a while. It may well be awful but the next one will taste better.

one-person show – a monodrama. Also known as the derogatory "Chair Theatre".

onstage – on the stage—visible to the audience.

Off Broadway – alternate theatre in New York City beginning in the 1950's.

Off-Off Broadway – small (90 seats), non-union theatre in New York City. This became "cutting-edge" after "Off Broadway" sold out to commercial interests.

Off-Off-Off Broadway – Sometimes a show in another city is jokingly called this.

offstage – (self-explanatory) Sometimes lines will be said offstage as indicated in the script.

open white – a lantern is said to be "in open white" if no filter or gel is used to colour its light.

opening night – when the run of a show begins. Characterized by much craziness backstage (and sometimes onstage). It is traditional for actors to exchange gifts and flowers on opening night.

opening night party – Remember actors have a show to give the next night. (See: "second night blues.")

opening night speech – Artistic Directors in many established theatres often give a speech to the audience on a premiere night before the curtain.

operators – the sound and lighting technicians who physically manipulate the cues from the booth under the direction of the stage manager.

orchestra pit – the space reserved for the musicians, usually the front part of the main floor.

overacting – acting unnaturally in an overly melodramatic way. Also called "Over The Top" (OTT) and "chewing the scenery".

P

pace – the speed and dramatic tempo of the performance.

PACT – Professional Association of Canadian Theatres.

page curtain – when an offstage stagehand or fellow actor holds the curtain open for an actor's entrance or exit.

pan – a bad review.

panorama – a large length of painted canvas depicting a distance landscape. This is unfurled across the back of the stage between two cylinders and can be manipulated so as to present a continually changing scene.

panto (pantomime) – traditional British vaudevillian children's show often presented at Christmas, featuring bad jokes, puns, songs, sexual innuendo, and an older male actor in drag.

paper tech – a meeting between director, designers and stage management to define and record the series of technical events required to operate the production. This would be done prior to tech week.

papering the house – offering free tickets to audience members to fill the house. Other than on opening night—not a good sign. Yet sadly very common.

party piece – a well-worn audition monologue. Actors are sometimes known to drag these out at parties.

patch – to connect a circuit to a dimmer.

patch bay – the board on which one connects circuits to dimmers.

pause – a much abused stage direction—a silence within the text. Though silence speaks volumes too.

paying your dues – young actors must endure less than enjoyable employment during their rise to the top. (See: Children's Theatre)

payoff line – a punch-line.

perch – a place for hanging lanterns on the side wall of the theatre auditorium. Also a place on the set where an actor can sit. "Can I perch here?"

periaktoi – three-sided flats that can be rotated to depict three different scenes. Often manipulated by actors.

"Featherweight"

SUPERSTITION: Peacock feathers are considered bad luck on stage – probably because they moult easily and the feathers can be inhaled by the actor.

peanut gallery – a group of hecklers.

peep-hole – some drop curtains have this so that actors can stare out into the audience during pre-show without being seen.

"Hi, Mom!"

SUPERSTITION: The peep-hole should always be at the center of the curtain. Looking at the audience from either side of the stage causes bad mojo. Some believe that the simple act of looking at the audience during pre-show is bad luck.

performance art – a "modern" but now very out of fashion non-linear style of performance more closely resembling a live art installation. (derogatory) A disjointed, over-the-top and pointless style of theatre that may feature outrageous stunts such as hurling raw liver into the audience.

period piece – a play that is set in a specific historical period. Not contemporary.

phoning it in – (…from the pub) a lackadaisical performance. Someone going through the motions of a performance.

photo-call – cast call so that production photographs may be taken. The director will have prepared a shot list and the actors may be asked to change costumes depending on the desired set up.

pick up cues – a director's note to speed up the response to a line without necessarily speaking faster, (or eating one's lines).

pick up pace – a director's note to quicken the speed and energy of a scene.

pimp –setting up a really funny joke.

pin spot – either a small (usually 100W) spotlight used for special effects (i.e. with a mirror ball) or, more usually in the theatre, a follow-spot with its iris diaphragm closed to its smallest diameter to illuminate, for instance, just a face.

pinteresque – (derogatory) extended "pregnant" pauses and endless repetition of words that cause the pace of a play to come to a screeching halt.

piss artist – an actor who is often drunk. Not professional.

pit – the area below the front of the stage. May be used to house the orchestra. Also called Orchestra Pit. Place historically for spectators who couldn't afford seats.

pit singer – a member of the cast who sings but is not seen onstage, usually to provide vocal backup.

places – the request for cast and crew to take their positions at the start of the performance.

plaster line – an imaginary line that runs across the proscenium along the upstage side of the proscenium wall. This line is used by designers and technicians to position various technical elements in the theatre.

playbill – a theatre programme. Also a poster.

playwright – the writer of a play.

Playwrights Guild of Canada – the Canadian association for professional and aspiring playwrights.

plot – 1. a play's storyline. 2. Also a lighting term: the actual brightness settings of each lantern and the LX cues. 3. Also used to describe the process of setting the cues. 4. Can also be used as an alternative for "blocking", i.e. setting the actors in their positions on-stage at an early stage in rehearsal.

post – a natural end to a specific section within a text. Posts don't necessarily happen at the end of a scene. They may indicate a new dramatic direction within a scene.

post-mortem – a meeting to discuss how the production went after a show has closed. This is used as a learning opportunity.

post-show blues – the general depression that comes after a show closes and unemployment looms.

practical – adjective used to describe properties or scenery which have to work as in real life when used; e.g. a practical kettle must actually heat up when switched on by an actor.

pre-production – the preparatory time period before a show goes into rehearsal.

preset – 1. (stage) the set up for the show with all props, set and quick-change costumes in place. 2. Also a lighting state—the light that appears on a set as the audience is walking in to the theatre.

pre-show music – the music or sound the audience hears while walking into the house. The walking out music is called "post-show." (Often the set returns to pre-set state.)

preview – a public performance given before the official opening. Often these are rehearsals with an audience, and a time when new material is tested and tried. (Usually one gets a discount for these performances.) The bigger the budget, the more previews there are. There is often a rehearsal scheduled on the afternoon of a preview night.

prima donna – leading female soloist in an opera company. (derogatory) A vain, conceited, temperamental performer of any gender.

principal (and principal boy) – a leading part in a play.

problem play – this usually refers to one of Shakespeare's less popular or less critically renowned shows (such as *Pericles*). An inferior play with plot problems. Some of Shakespeare's problem plays are undeserving of this title. Blood-soaked, fast-moving, raunchy plays like *Titus Andronicus* were labelled as such by stuffed-shirt Victorian academics and that smear has stuck ever since.

producer – the person in charge of the funding and budget of the show.

production – the specific version of a show.

production desk – a table set up in the house to accommodate the needs of stage manager, lighting designer and operators during tech week. This will disappear as dress rehearsals begin.

production manager – the person in charge of the physical aspects of the show from costing the set to hiring carpenters.

production week – the final week before dress rehearsal where the show comes together in the theatre.

programme – pamphlet handed to the audience containing information about all the fine people who have worked very hard on the show.

programmed sound – when the action onstage is piped to any other room in the theatre. Programmed sound can be piped to the booth, the green room and the artistic director's office. Be aware of programmed sound as casual conversations on stage may be heard by many… (See "gossip.")

projecting – vocalization using the diaphragm in order to be heard without shouting. Actors are becoming less and less adept at this with the advent of stage microphones or lavs.

projections – slides or video used in a production.

prologue – a brief scene or speech given at the beginning of a play.

prompt – to help an actor with his lines when he either asks or is stumbling.

prompt book – the binder kept by the stage manager that contains all paperwork necessary to the production of the play, including a script with blocking and cues. The prompt book is usually left at the theatre during the run of the play and is turned in to the producing theatre company at the end of the run. (Also "prompt script.") See "The Book."

prompter – amateur companies almost always have a prompter, someone who sits in the wings and prompts the actors if they forget their lines. There is no such position in the professional theatre. Pros should not forget lines! Neither should amateurs, for that matter, but it happens.

prop table – the table backstage where props are laid out, usually in a detailed mapped out order. It is important to keep it neat and to return props to it after they are used.

properties – small items which actors carry onto or around the stage. Also used loosely for "set dressing". Usually abbreviated to props.

property master (or mistress) – person responsible for the obtaining of and/or construction of the props.

proscenium – the outlining frame of the stage opening that separates the house from the stage. Also called the Proscenium Arch.

proscenium style – method of stage movement and position to make the most of the proscenium viewpoint. Positioning the body to face the audience while acting with other characters onstage.

protagonist – originally the principal actor in Greek drama. It has since come to mean the hero of a play or central focus character who drives the plot forward.

in the public domain – said of a play that is no longer under the protection of copyright laws, and which can be performed without payment of royalties.

publicist – the person who markets the show to the public and arranges photo calls, interviews, etc.

punch line – payoff line to a joke.

punters – the public. (See also: "bums in seats" and "audience.")

PWYC – Pay What You Can—no fixed ticket price. Usually for matinees and Tuesday nights.

pyrotechnics – usually abbreviated to "pyro". The use of explosions, flashes, smoke, etc. onstage.

Q

quick change – a fast costume change often with the assistance of an ASM, dresser, or fellow actor. Usually there are rehearsals just for this.

quick change booth – makeshift backstage dressing rooms used for quick changes of costumes, wigs, etc.; it may be used by different actors at different times during the show.

R

rake – many stage floors, usually in theatres built for dance or variety, are higher at the back than at the front, to give the audience a better view. These stages are said to be "raked", and the "rake" is the angle of slope from back to front. This is where the terms "upstage" and "downstage" come from. The angle of the rake is of great concern to Equity due to health and safety rules. In many modern theatres it is the audience seating that is raked, not the stage.

rats – child actors (originally from *The Nutcracker*—children who play the rat army soldiers). In French "Les Rats".

read-through – usually the first rehearsal at which the company reads through the script without stopping.

realism – a theatre movement of the late 19th century; a faithful depiction of real-life situations and characters onstage. Less extreme than Naturalism.

rear elevation – the scale drawing that gives a back view of the set.

rehearsal – practice, practice, practice. (In French: "Repetition")

rehearsal hall – a large empty practice space. The floor will often be taped with the dimensions of the set by the stage management team before the first rehearsal.

rehearsal notes – the stage manager's summation of the day to be sent to the entire production and technical team. These are crucial to the different departments to keep updated on changes made during the actors' rehearsal.

rehearsal props – mock props that give an actor a chance to work with something while the real thing is being bought or built. Also sometimes rehearsal costumes are needed in the case of skirts, shoes, capes etc.

remount – a show that receives a new production run requiring a briefer rehearsal period than the original. If the majority of actors are not returning and mostly new actors need to be rehearsed, it may technically not be a remount.

repertory – a company of actors which performs more than one play in a given period, alternating from one play to another. Shortens to "Rep".

reprise – musical term: to repeat, in whole or in part, a song which has already been sung in the show.

resting – unemployed.

reveal – (noun) a surprise that appears onstage.

review – a published critique of a play. A review will sometimes give a brief plot synopsis.

reviewer – a commonplace critic.

revolve – a stage or, more usually, part of a stage, which can revolve through 360 degrees.

revue – a musical entertainment of unrelated songs, dances, and sketches.

rhyming couplet – (Shakespearean) two lines of verse that rhyme at the end, usually signalling the end of a scene. ie, Hamlet: "The play's the thing wherein I'll catch the conscience of the king."

rhubarb – extras will often mutter this word over and over to fill in sound in large group scenes. It works.

rig – 1. a lighting term. To set the lanterns in position. 2. As a noun, its refers to the actual positioning of the lanterns.

rigging – the way in which mobile scenery is controlled.

riser – a platform to perform on (usually 4' x 8' x 6" height.) Often a combination of several risers is used in a set design.

role – a character that the actor plays.

rostrum -- a moveable platform. (Plural: rostra.)

rule of three – a comedy term. Most often, jokes are told in three parts. Also, running gags will often be repeated three times for maximum comic effect. (For some reason the fourth time won't be funny.)

run – the total number of performances for a production.

run-through – a rehearsal performance from beginning to end without stopping.

running crew – the backstage group of people who perform all the technical tasks during the show.

running gag – (also "running joke") a joke that repeats itself at various points in a performance.

running lights – low wattage lights for backstage, usually a low-watt blue that won't cast light onto the stage.

running order – the order in which a show's scenes and songs are performed.

running time – a play's timed duration.

S

safety curtain – a curtain of fireproofed material (once upon a time it was asbestos) usually with a metal frame which covers the entire proscenium opening and acts as a firebreak between the stage and the auditorium. Known as the "iron"—when it is raised or lowered, the theatrical term is "Iron going in (or out.)"

sand bucket – a backstage receptacle for extinguishing prop cigarettes. Also a handy place for an actor to vomit just before going onstage. (See butterflies.)

satire – a comedy in which contemporary public vice and folly are exposed to ridicule.

scenario – a synopsis of a dramatic work. A loose plot description.

scene – one section of a play. Usually divided by time or setting.

scene/character breakdown – a chart indicating each scene in a play, with all page numbers, necessary actors listed and some indication of the action and setting.

scene dock – backstage area for storing scenery and other sundries.

scene shift – 1. the process of moving from one setting into another during a play. 2. Also to move (shift) a prop or piece of furniture.

scene work – rehearsal that is devoted to the exploration of a given scene. Ideally only the actors who are in the scene are called for this work.

scenography – a term used when the movement of the scenery is choreographed and a part of the storytelling.

Scottish Play (The) – See *Macbeth*. This phrase tries to avoid the curse.

scrim – loosely-woven material that is used as a backdrop. When lit from the front scrim is opaque, when lit from behind it is transparent.

score – a written musical arrangement.

season – the group of plays that a theatre will be presenting within a designated time period.

second-acting – a practice of unscrupulous (or poverty-stricken) theatre-lovers. Second-acting is mingling outside of the theatre with the audience during intermission and then sneaking in to the theatre to see Act II for free.

second night blues – notoriously low energy performance due to a less friendly audience and/or too much partying the night before. (See "opening night party.")

set – the scenery for a particular show or individual scene.

set designer – creates the scenic aspects of the production. Lighting design is a separate task although he/she will work closely with the lighting designer.

set dressing – items on a set which are not actually used by anyone but which make it look more realistic (e.g. curtains over a window, a bowl of flowers on a table, and so on).

sheet of lies – slang for an acting resume. It is actually unwise to lie about one's stage accomplishments on a resume. The theatre community is a very small and interconnected family.

"Frightening Footwear"

SUPERSTITION: Putting character shoes on a table or chair in the dressing room is considered very bad luck. Also, if your shoes squeak while you are making your first entrance, it is a sure sign that you will be well received by the audience. If you kick off your shoes and they both land on their soles there will be good luck in a performance. If they don't then there will be disaster.

---

showboat – stealing a scene with a large boasting performance.

showcase – (*American*) a play performed for free to theatrical backers, agents, producers etc. Actors may actually pay to be in these productions. It's an indication of how difficult it is for actors to get work… there are so many of them competing for so few paying jobs.

show crush – a short-term romance, admiration, or close friendship that usually ends with the production's final show.

show and tell – the presentation given by designers of the set model and costume designs shown to the members of the ensemble on the first day of rehearsal. A time to ask questions and advance common mission.

show stopper – an outstanding performance that literally stops the show because of audience applause.

shtick – (*Yiddish*) comedic/goofy stage business. Derogatory: An actor's well-worn stage tricks.

sides – (*Elizabethan*) an excerpt from a play that focuses on one character's lines. The term "sides" was originally singular—"side" meaning "part." Scripts were hand-written with great speed—often just containing one set of lines to save time and paper. It has since become more of a film term meaning a condensed form of the day's shooting script.

sightlines – viewing angles that determine what is visible to the audience on stage and what is not.

sign-in sheet – on arriving at the theatre pre-performance the cast must sign this sheet in order to let the stage manager know that they are in the theatre and ready to go.

sitzprobe – (musical) first full rehearsal for performers and orchestra. Text and score only, no blocking.

skirt – the downstage edge of the stage.

slam – a bad review.

slip stage – a platform on wheels or casters that moves on and off stage during the course of a play to facilitate rapid scene changes. Also called Wagon and Jackknife Stage.

smash hit – a wildly popular production.

soliloquy – a dramatic form of discourse in which a character talks to himself or herself or reveals his or her thoughts without addressing a listener. Sometimes addressed directly to the audience.

soap-boxing – (derogatory) a playwright will sometimes use the characters of his play to spout his own political opinions.

soft goods – drops made of cloth.

sold right out – the three best words in the theatrical lexicon.

sound designer – the person who puts together the found music or sound-scape for a show.

sound effects – live or pre-recorded sound during the show.

space – generic term for a performing or rehearsing place.

spacing – when rehearsing in the theatre for the first time after being used to the rehearsal hall one may have to adjust certain movement given unforeseen discrepancies in the physicality of the set and stage. Also, generally the performance will have to get bigger, allowing for the audience to become a part of the interpretation. This is common practice while touring to different venues.

spear carrier – (derogatory) a minor role without lines. An extra. A supernumerary. If it's a paying job, congratulations.

special – a lighting instrument not used for general illumination but for a special effect, such as lighting a single actor in one place during a monologue. It is important to hit one's mark properly or you will miss the special.

special skills – final section of a resume listing non-acting talents—such as horseback riding, archery, kung fu, etc. If these skills are exaggerated it may lead to trouble. (see "sheet of lies.")

spike mark – a mark on the stage or rehearsal floor, usually a piece of tape, that denotes the specific placement of a piece of scenery or a prop. To place the spike mark is "to spike".

spill – extraneous light that can be cut off with a shutter.

spirit gum – the glue that adheres fake beards, etc. Can be painful to sensitive skin.

spitter – an actor who sprays saliva when he speaks his lines. This is sometimes the result of stage jitters—as is the opposite, "cotton mouth".

spoon feed – giving exhaustive acting/staging notes to an actor who is not making choices or doing their work.

spotlight – (or simply, "spot") a type of lantern whose beam is focused through a lens or series of lenses to make it more controllable.

SRO – "standing room only" (also "sold right out"). Music to the ears of any producer.

stage – the playing area. Where it all happens.

stage acting – a broader acting method, usually fairly large so the distant audience can enjoy the performance.

stage brace – an adjustable piece of stage equipment that fits into a brace cleat to support scenery.

stage crew – theatre staff who undertake duties backstage.

stage directions – a playwright's instructions indicating the movement or stage business of the characters or other descriptions of the physical setting or atmosphere of the play. Traditionally, stage directions in a script would be followed to the letter. Any variation and the director would run the risk of a nasty letter from the playwright or his/her surviving relatives. But these days, the playwright's stage directions are often ignored.

stage door – a back entrance to the theatre where you meet the fans after the show.

stage door johnny – a hopeful fan who hangs around the actors' entrance, hoping to catch a glimpse of (or the eye of) an actress, or actor.

stage fight – a choreographed combat for the stage, with or without weapons. Must be very well rehearsed.

stage fright – happens to all actors at some point. See also: "butterflies", "jitters."

stage hand – stage crew.

stage left – when facing the audience, the area of the stage on the actor's left.

stage manager – (SM) the hub of a production. One can't really see the huge amount of work they do but suffice it to say they are the first and last voice one should hear at rehearsal and the one to go to with any concerns regarding schedule, props, costume—everything. They run the show and can give notes after the show has opened. Good ones think the world of actors and will fiercely stand up for their rights. Never underestimate the stage manager's artistic opinion.

stage manager's desk – the table in rehearsal where stage management sits in order to run the rehearsal. Supplied with pencils, water and tissues, it is a place actors respect.

stage mother – a domineering parent who pushes his/her children into becoming performers.

stage prank – there is usually at least one practical joker in any play. Stage pranks involve hiding costumes and props, trying to fit unusual words into the text, upstaging other actors, replacing onstage drinks with real booze, etc. Stage pranks usually come late in a long run. Stage pranks can be dangerous and are considered very unprofessional. This

however doesn't prevent even seasoned professionals from engaging in them.

stage presence – being awake and alive on stage. May denote someone who has great charisma or watchability.

stage right – when facing the audience, the area of the stage on the actor's right.

stage whisper – a loud whisper on stage for the benefit of the audience.

stakes – an actor's term that refers to the importance of a character's personal investment or concern within a specific scene.

standing ovation – if an audience is suitably impressed with a play it will rise to its feet and applaud at the ending. A standing ovation is not guaranteed in the theatre. The propensity for an audience to give a standing ovation depends on the calibre of the performance, of course, but also varies greatly from audience to audience and city to city.

star trap – a trapdoor in the stage used for surprise entrances.

star turn – a stand-out performance.

starter's pistol – a prop gun(hopefully) filled with blanks – used for offstage gunshots. Always count on these to misfire. The unfortunate ASM will then have to yell "BANG!"

state – a lighting term, referring to the state of lighting at a particular moment in the play.

status – in any scene, one character will have more power than the other. That power will often shift during the course of the play. The character with power is said to be "high status" the character without it is "low status".

stealing the show – said of an actor whose performance outshines all others. Often a featured role rather than a lead.

stealing focus – when something happens onstage that takes the audience's eyes off what was intended and rehearsed. Unprofessional if purposefully done by a fellow actor.

step unit – a three or four stair riser (approximately 24 inches high).

straight man – a member of a double act who plays a stooge, feed, or comic foil in theatrical comedy. An actor who is surprised by, or is the object of, a joke by the comic actor.

stratford swivel (The) – craning the neck in every direction to scan the immediate area to ensure that no one is within earshot before partaking in malicious gossip. Important in the bar.

straw hat – summer theatre or semi-professional theatre.

strike – the removal of all stage equipment, scenery, props, lights, and costumes from the stage area after production. (See also "Take Down")

striplight – a long, narrow lighting instrument used for a general wash of light. This trough-like instrument may be sunk in the floor permanently or may be mobile.

strobe – a lantern which emits a regular, controllable series of high-power flashes rather than continuous light. Strobes can induce epileptic fits and so warning about their use should always be stated on lobby signage, in the program and verbally before the show starts.

stumble through – an early stage run-through. (See also: Crash 'n Burn.)

substitution – a rehearsal technique that substitutes the actor's personal experience with a character's. (So if the actor has to die onstage, he/she might imagine the more familiar feeling of being plunged into a bath of ice-cold water.) See also: "affective memory."

subtext – what the character says may not be what he means. Subtext is the meaning or desire behind the words. Or, in the back of the mind.

summer stock – traditional summer theatre—light entertainment for cottagers.

supernumerary – opera term for an extra.

supporting role – a secondary character

superstition – the theatre is very old and has many superstitions. Theatre folk take them very seriously so if one decides to make fun, prepare to be punished. Theatre superstitions primarily concern luck—good or bad—in performance. Just like a baseball player.

swatch – a small piece of fabric or paint used to demonstrate the color and/or texture of the material being used.

sweet spot – a place on the stage with particularly good acoustics. Best place to be heard by an audience. Thanks to the peculiar acoustics of some theatres, this is not always downstage centre.

swing – a scheduled substitute actor. Most often used in musicals.

T

table work – early reading and discussion of the play before the actors get on their feet to begin staging. A time to ask questions and get to know the play.

tableau – a still freeze created by actors for a striking visual effect.

tabs – the curtains which close across the proscenium arch are called "House Tabs".

tab dressing – light on the House Tabs (see "Tabs") before the curtain goes up and during the intermission.

tank – a show "tanks" when it has a brief/disastrous run.

Tannoy – an old-fashioned backstage speaker brand name. (See "programmed sound.") Important for those actors in the Green Room to keep track of what is happening on stage.

teaser – black fabric that is hung to mask lamps.

tech day – a day when the cast is called to work only on technical aspects of a play.

tech director – the person in charge of all technical aspects of a production.

tech dress – a rehearsal with costume that may be stopped by the stage manager if a technical cue needs to be practiced again.

technical rehearsal – the rehearsal or series of rehearsals in which the technical elements of the show are integrated with the work of actors.

tech run – a run-through of the play using technical elements.

tech week – the work week before opening.

technician – general term for theatre operators and crew. They do not like being called "techies". (See: "IATSE.")

telegraph – over-emphasizing the set-up of a joke so that it's too obvious to the audience as to what's coming.

ten out of twelve – during tech week, a twelve-hour workday with two hours of meal breaks.

The Show Must Go On! - No, it doesn't. See "fire marshal".

text work – work that is done in the early part of rehearsal to make sure everyone knows what is happening in the play.

thank you – part of stage ettiquette. Thank the ASM for setting a prop, the wardrobe person for taking care of one's costumes and the stage manager for giving one one's show call. In Denmark at the end of the day the members of a theatre company say goodbye to each other with "Tak for dag!" literally, thank you for the day.

theater – American spelling of "theatre".

theatre – playwright George S. Kaufman called the theatre a "fabulous invalid"—always in intensive care but never quite dead.

theatre cat – many old theatres have them. Used to control the theatre mouse population; they are often named after a Shakespearean character ("Hamlet" "Puck" etc). Some believe that theatre cats outrank playwrights in the theatre hierarchy.

> *"Mouse Insurance"*
>
> **SUPERSTITION: Theatre cats are considered good luck. But if one crosses the stage during a performance then misfortune is sure to follow. Bad luck will also come to those who kick a theatre cat.**

Theatre of Cruelty – a form of drama developed in 1935 by Antonin Artaud in parallel with the Grand-Guignol and Surrealist movements. The "Cruelty" meant here is the strain of the audience during the performance, which should be aesthetically shocked with the cooperation of staging, sound and lighting elements. To this day, artists see this as an opportunity to abuse the audience with bad/wacky performances. This is why so many contemporary audiences are turned off by experimental theatre.

Theatre of the Absurd – a form of drama that emphasizes the absurdity of human existence by employing disjointed, repetitious, and meaningless dialogue, purposeless and confusing situations, and plots that lack realistic or logical development.

There are no small parts, only small actors. – the standard rebuke by a director to an actor who is complaining about the small size of his/her role. Also: "There are no small parts, only small paycheques." Also to fidgety onstage extras: "Don't just do something! Stand there!"

thespian – an actor. From the ancient Greek "Thespus"—who was the first actor to stride downstage and deliver solo lines separate from the chorus.

third eye – often an actor will be asked to get rid of his third eye, meaning he is not in the moment but is observing his own performance. Ideally that is what directors are for.

throw line – rope that is used to secure flats.

throw away line – an unimportant piece of text. Often used in a moment where the character's subtext is more important than the actual line.

thrust – a type of stage that projects out into the auditorium and has audience seated on three sides.

thumbnail – (from "thumbnail sketch") a small but distinctive role.

toi-toi – the opera version of "break a leg". An imaginary kiss on both cheeks.

tomatoes – (rotten) traditional fruit that is hurled at the stage by the disgruntled audience.

top of show – the first cue.

tornado curtain – a shocking plot revelation just before the curtain drops for intermission. This ensures that the audience will return for the second act.

tough house – a difficult audience.

touring company – a theatre troupe that presents plays at a series of different venues.

touring house – a theatrical venue that often hosts touring productions. Also called a "road house".

tracks – the rails on which curtains (tabs) run.

tragedy – a sad play. Classically it is the royalty who has a great downfall. As opposed to comedy when it is the common folk who meet their destiny.

trail off lines – lines that drift off into silence.

transparency – gauze or thin fabric, which when painted and lit from the front appears to be a normally painted cloth – but when lit from behind becomes transparent.

trap – removable area of the stage floor that allows access to the area underneath the stage. There are many different types of traps.

traveller – a curtain that can open to the sides of the stage.

treading the boards – acting. (Also "hitting the boards.")

treading on the laughs – cutting off audience reaction to a joke or bit of comic business. This often happens on opening night when the actors are unaccustomed to performing in front of an audience. Also, "stepping on" or "killing" the laughs.

trick line – thin black line that is used for sight gags and magically moved objects.

trilogy – a series of three plays on a related theme or storyline.

trim – the height to which a piece of scenery or stage equipment will be flown.

trouser role – a character part that calls for a woman to dress as a man (Viola from *Twelfth Night*). Also pants roll, breeches role.

truck – a rostrum or platform on wheels, on which scenery can be mounted so that it can be rolled into any position on-stage.

turkey – a terrible play. Also "gobbler", "cranberry sauce", etc. (see also bomb, flop, dog).

turntable – portion of the stage that revolves. Also called a revolve

TV acting – (derogatory) mumbly, inaudible stage acting.

twist lock – a type of connector on a lamp that twists to connect

two-hander – a play with only two people. (Not to be confused with a "two-acter"—a play with two acts.)

twofer – a connector for two lamps to plug into one.

TYA – "Theatre for Young Audiences"—culturally updated version of "Children's Theatre".

U

understudy – replacement actor in case of emergency. In a big cast it will often be filled by a cast member with a smaller role in the same production.

understudy rehearsals – often done after the show has opened. The understudy is supposed to copy the main actor's performance as opposed to interpreting it themselves.

union house – a theatre that only employs certified IATSE technicians and labourers.

unit – a section of the script.

unit set – a set that can serve as several different settings by changing only one or two set pieces, or by adding different set dressing.

unities (The) – *(ancient Greek)* Aristotle's disciplined structure of three "unities" for any play: unity of place, unity of time, and unity of action. The play should be in one location. Action in the play should take place during one day. All action should be focused toward one specific purpose.

upstage – 1. at the back of the stage; away from the audience. 2. As a verb: when one actor deliberately draws the attention of the audience to himself for purely selfish purposes. 3. In a proscenium, actors who move upstage force fellow actors to face away from the audience. 4. Inadvertently stealing focus is also called upstaging. It is also possible to upstage oneself…

usher – front of house staff who distribute programmes and seat patrons.

USL – upstage left.

USR – upstage right.

V

valuables – thieves are fond of stealing wallets and jewellery from dressing rooms. The stage manager will often collect wallets and jewellery for safe keeping while the show is on. David Mamet says that the best direction you can ever give to an actor is to advise him to take his wallet onstage. We are of the opinion that Blackberrys, iPhones and laptops should also be submitted, as the current trend to "connect" with friends during a performance is unprofessional, vile and impolite.

vamp – a repeated passage of music to cover a performer's stage business or personal rhythm as worked out with the music director. Can also be most helpful as a stop-gap to cover miscues.

vanity production – (derogatory) a play that is self-funded, self-produced and self-performed by an individual who would not be hired otherwise.

Vaudeville – a mixture of songs, comic sketches, dance, magic and animal acts popularized in the late 1800s.

velours – curtains hung both to mask the backstage area and to shape the onstage area. Also called blacks.

venue – the place where the performance takes place.

vocal masque – a collage performance on a specific theme that may contain voice, movement, singing, dancing.

voice over – a disembodied voice broadcast live or pre-recorded.

W

walk-on – a small role with no lines. Often a celebrity cameo that only needs a brief rehearsal before the performance.

walk the stage – during tech—having someone stand on stage for a lighting focus. (See "hot walker.")

wandelprobe – the first fully blocked rehearsal with performers and orchestra.

wardrobe – 1. costumes required for a particular production. 2. The department that makes and takes care of costumes.

warm up – before rehearsal and before a show. Helps prepare the voice and body as well as get focused for the work at hand.

wash – light used to give a general illumination of the stage; quite often a specific colour is used in a wash. Commonly called a General Wash. Often denoted by temperature: reds and yellows denote a warm wash. Blues or whites represent a cold wash.

well-made play – a play with a cleverly constructed plot. (derogatory) Lacking in characterization. Old-fashioned.

"Don't whistle while you work."

SUPERSTITION: Whistling in a theatre is considered very bad luck. Probably originated from navvy stage-hands. A whistle would signal the dropping of a sandbag from the flies.

wigs – hairpieces. They can be very fickle, almost as bad as fake moustaches.

"Flip It!"

SUPERSTITION: Certain wigs can bring good luck. Actors will sometimes wear them even though the part doesn't call for it. Changing wigs for a performance is considered bad luck.

wings – the sides of the stage, out of sight of the audience, where actors stand before making their entrance and where props are kept, ready to be brought onto the stage.

"with the fairies" – staggeringly drunk. "I'm with the fairies now…"

working drawings – drawings to scale that give specifics of both set and prop construction.

work lights – used for general illumination of the stage when not in performance.

work call – a time period during which the crew is called to work on any technical element of a production without actors or rehearsal.

workshop – development stage of a play. Uses actors to read the play.

workshopitis – workshopping a play to death without a production in sight.

World's Second Oldest Profession (The) – there are many pretenders to this title (undertaking, journalism, etc.) but in truth, it is the acting profession.

The oldest profession is prostitution. However some would say there isn't much of a difference between the two.

"Revolving Doors"

SUPERSTITION: **It is an omen of failure for an actor to choose the wrong door when searching for a theatre manager or agent's office.**

X

x-ray – one should demand one of these if one falls off the stage in a blackout.

Y

"Bad Banana"

SUPERSTITION: **Certain shades of yellow in a costume, prop, or musical instrument are considered bad luck.**

yes and… – an improv exercise. Performers have to accept and then add to whatever another performer suggests. (e.g.: "I heard you got married." "Yes, and it's a gorilla.")

Z

zanni – servant characters in Commedia dell-arte. This is where the word "zany" comes from.

Sue Miner is versed in both classical text and new works. She is co-artistic director (with husband Mark Brownell) of Pea Green Theatre Group, has garnered several Dora nominations, been thrice nominated for the Pauline McGibbon Award for body of work in direction and was touted as one of Toronto's Top-10 theatre artists by *Now Magazine*. She is also a 2010 Harold Indie Theatre Award winner.

Mark Brownell is a Toronto-based playwright whose body of work includes the Governor General's Award nominated *Monsieur d'Eon*, the Dora Award-winning *Iron Road*, *High Sticking* (Scirocco Drama, 2006), *The Martha Stewart Projects*, *The Barbeque King*, and *Medici Slot Machine* (Scirocco Drama, 2008).